inventions WHY?

WHY IS NICKEL SO POPULAR IN BATTERIES?

An imprint of Om Books International

WHY?

CONTENTS

Find out!

What happens when you divide a number by zero?

1 Why was the number zero invented?

The number zero was invented independently by the Indians and the Mayans. Before the invention of zero, people used an empty space to indicate its value. This was confusing because an empty space was also used as a separator between numbers. To avoid confusion, people started using a dot to represent zero, which eventually took the form of the number zero that we use today.

Pocket fact

The arithmometer!
The arithmometer was the first commercially successful calculating machine. It could perform all four basic operations — addition, subtraction, multiplication and division. It was invented by Charles Xavier Thomas de Colmar in1820.

2 Why are the numbers on a calculator reversed?

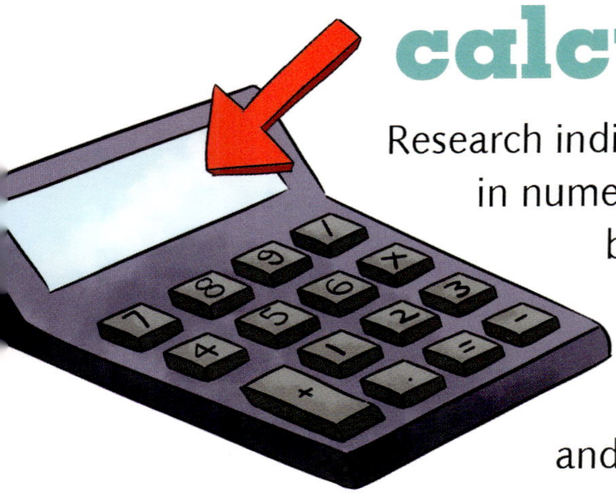

Research indicates that zero is the most commonly used number in numerical calculations. Pressing it repeatedly would not be convenient if it was placed in the middle of the number pad, and it would invariably result in errors. This is the reason zero is kept at the bottom of the calculator and the numbers 1, 2 and 3 are placed near it.

3 Why did the earliest forks have only two tines?

They were not used for dining! Forks were invented in Europe, thousands of years ago. The earlier forks had only two tines. These forks were used as agricultural and kitchen tools. Later on, people started using forks to eat food. However, this became a problem because diners often accidentally injured themselves with it. To solve this problem, the number of tines on the forks was increased. Nowadays, forks with four tines are considered most comfortable for use by diners.

Find out!

What is cutlery?

Pocket fact

Not just a pinch of salt!
Salt is used as a food preservative because bacteria cannot grow in salty conditions. Salt was used as an effective preservative even in the ancient times and this made it a precious commodity back in the day.

4 Why were food preservatives invented?

To preserve food for longer durations and prevent it from getting spoiled! Food preservation is said to have enabled ancient people to settle down and form a community. The ancient preservation methods included salting, fermentation, oil packing, pickling and smoking. The technique of canning food was discovered in the 19th century by Nicholas Apert.

5 Why were stickers invented?

For advertisement and for use as postage stamps and tax stamps! A sticker refers to an adhesive label. The exact information about the invention of stickers remains unknown. It is said that they were first used by Egyptians to advertise their daily market rates. They were also used as postage stamps and tax stamps. R. Stanton Avery is said to have invented the first self-adhesive label in the 1930s.

Find out!

Where has the word pencil been derived from?

6 Why is pencil lead called lead?

As graphite was mistaken for lead! Pencil lead is made of graphite. When graphite was first discovered in England in the form of a large, solid black mass, it was thought to be black lead. People used sticks of graphite for marking. The sticks were so brittle that they could be used only after they were wrapped in sheep skin or put into hollowed-out wood sticks. This led to the invention of pencil. And till date the inner marking portion of a pencil is referred to as lead.

Pocket fact

Bumper Stickers!
Bumper stickers were invented by a printer named Forest Gill. They were made for advertising Rocky Mountain's Rock City attraction.

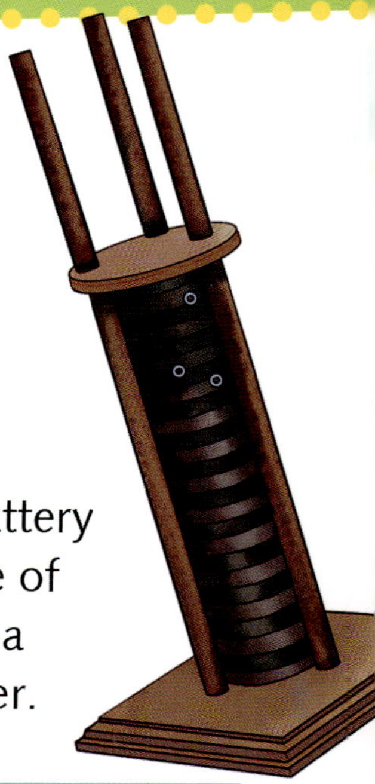

7 Why was the first battery called the voltaic pile?

It was named after its inventor! Voltaic pile is the first ever battery invented by the Italian scientist Alessandro Volta. It was a pile of discs made from copper and zinc. Each pile was separated by a piece of leather or cardboard soaked in weak acid or salt water. Volta found that electricity flowed through the pile of discs and hence called it the voltaic pile.

Pocket fact

Benjamin Franklin was the first to use the word 'battery' in 1748. He used it in reference to Leyden jars. This word was borrowed from the military terminology.

8 Why is nickel so popular in batteries?

These batteries have a longer shelf life! Nickel is a metal that is widely used in batteries. Nickel-based batteries last longer as compared to the other batteries. They can be stored in a discharged state and can be transported easily. Also, nickel-based batteries can be recharged very quickly. These are low cost batteries and are available in a wide range of sizes.

Find out!

When was the first rechargeable battery invented?

9 Why did the first vacuum cleaners have wooden handles?

To move the bellows! The first vacuum cleaner was invented in the 1860s. It consisted of bellows that sucked dirt into the vacuum cleaner. It also had a wooden handle, which was moved back and forth to create vacuum in the tube to suck up dust. It was much later that electrically operated vacuum cleaners were invented.

Find out!

Name the first robotic vacuum cleaner.

Pocket fact

H.C. Booth got his inspiration to invent the vacuum cleaner while travelling on a train. He put a handkerchief across his mouth and sucked up as much dust into it as he could. The vacuum filter was invented shortly after.

10 Why wasn't the first electric vacuum cleaner successful?

Due to its complexity! The first electric vacuum cleaner was invented by Hubert Cecil Booth in 1901. It was in the form of a large, horse-drawn, petrol-driven unit. It blasted out the dust and blew it with compressed air into a receptacle; the dust was not sucked into the unit. These vacuum cleaners were not very portable.

11 Why were the first bicycles called boneshakers?

They juddered over every bump and road! therefore they were called 'boneshakers'. Bicycles were first invented in 1817 by the German nobleman Baron von Drais. These bicycles were made of wooden frames and iron wheels. They lacked pedals. The first pedal-driven bicycle was invented by Pierre Lallement in 1864. It had pedals and cranks on the front wheel to give simultaneous balance and power.

Find out!

Can you name all the parts of a bicycle? Give it a try!

12 Why were bicycle gears invented?

Pocket fact

Let's race!
One of the most famous bicycle races in the world is the Tour de France. It was established in 1903 and is considered to be the ultimate test of endurance.

To make cycling easy! In the 1800s, bicyclists had a difficult time cycling on hilly roads, as it was tough to pedal. In 1871, James Starley invented the Ariel which was probably the first geared bike. Bicycles with gears were invented so that bicyclists could pedal comfortably on any terrain. They could shift to an easier gear on upside roads or when riding into the wind. These gears do all the hard work of moving the chain from one sprocket (chain ring) to the next!

13

Why were Ford's Model T cars black?

Since black paint dried fast! Henry Ford's Model T car was first sold in 1908. It was sturdy, reliable and easy to drive. It became the first car to be mass-produced in 1913, with almost 10,000 cars manufactured each day. From 1914 to 1925, all the Model T cars manufactured were black in colour because black paint dried the quickest. This allowed the assembly line to operate at top speed and manufacture more cars!

Find out!

How much time does it take to change a Volkswagen Beetle's engine?

Pocket fact

The first Model T cars were sold for around $850! But their price fell to $260 by 1925.

14

Why was Volkswagen's Beetle named so?

Due to its bug-like shape! VW Beetle is one of the most popular cars manufactured by the Volkswagen Group. It is also known as the people's car. The Beetle got its name from its downward pointing front and curved back, which give it a bug-like shape. This streamlined shape reduces air resistance, resulting in lesser fuel consumption.

Find out!

What are modern-day inks made of?

15 Why were oil-based inks invented?

So that they don't blur when used in the press! Many ancient cultures around the world discovered and invented different kinds of ink. In ancient times, natural plants (plant dyes) or graphite ground with water were used as ink. But they tended to blur when used in printing. It was Gutenberg who developed an oil-based ink in the 15th century. It was made from soot, turpentine, walnut oil and unknown plant extracts. This ink was more resilient than water-based inks.

16 Why do 3D printers have heating elements?

To melt plastic! A 3D printer is a device that creates a three-dimensional model of an object. Many 3D printers have a heating element. This heating element is used to melt the material that is used in printing. The molten material is passed through a steel pipe to a nozzle. The layers of this material are shaped into the desired object, which solidifies quickly after coming out of the printer.

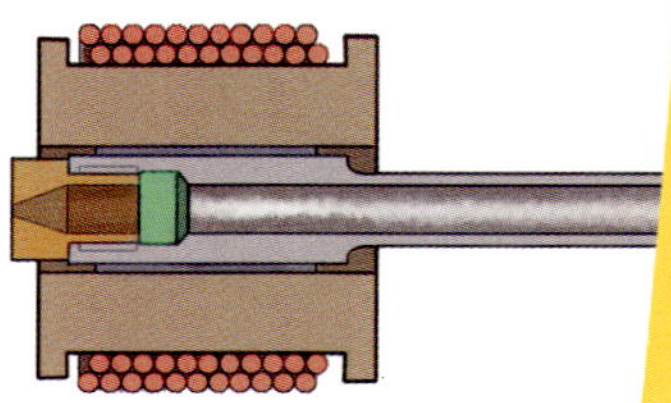

Pocket fact

Roots of 3D printing!
In 1984, Chuck Hull invented a process called 'stereolithography'. In this process, UV lasers were used to solidify photopolymers that created 3D parts layer by layer.

17 Why were windmills a common sight in olden days?

They were used to pump water and for many other works! Windmills are used to generate energy which can be used in many ways. In olden days, windmills made work easier. They were used for pumping water, grinding grains and spices and sawing wood. They were a common sight in agricultural fields prior to the invention of modern agricultural implements.

Find out!

Which one of these produces electricity-wind turbines or wind mills?

Pocket fact

That's tall!
The largest wind turbine in the world is located in Hawaii. It is 20-storey tall and has blades the length of a football field.

18 Why don't we use waterwheels anymore?

Waterwheel is a huge wheel driven by flowing water. When water is flowed over it, it moves. In olden days, the energy produced from water wheels was used for different purposes such as milling flour, grinding wood, pounding fibre for cloth making and so on. But these machines were dependent on flowing water. They could be located only near flowing water bodies. So they were replaced by smaller, less expensive turbines, which generated hydroelectricity.

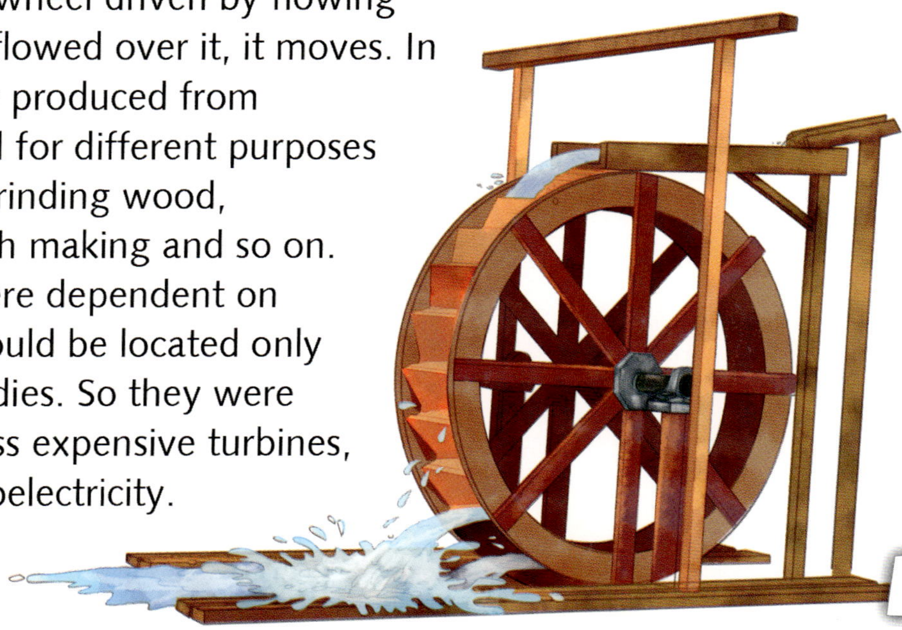

> **Find out!**
>
> Use the principle of 'camera obscura' and make a pinhole camera with the help of your parents.

19 Why was camera obscura called a dark room?

In the ancient times when there were no cameras, the principle of camera obscura was used to reflect images. In Latin 'camera' means room and 'obscura' means dark, hence the name 'dark room'. It refers to a dark room with a small hole in one wall. On the wall opposite to the hole, an upside-down image of the object outside is formed. This was first recorded by the Chinese philosopher Mo-Ti in the 5th century BC. He called this darkened room a 'collecting place' or the 'locked treasure room'.

> **Pocket fact**
>
> Say cheese!
> Clicking photographs wasn't always the simple routine we follow today. Early cameras were so slow that it would take several hours to actually capture a film!

20 Why did camera reels go out of fashion?

They were replaced by digital cameras! The first cameras used reels that were developed into photographs. However, with the invention of the digital camera, people stopped using cameras with reels. The reason behind this was the easy distribution, easy transport, low cost and high clarity of the photographs taken with digital cameras. Also, reels can get spoilt due to scratches and tears but digital photographs retain their quality for a much longer duration.

21 Why were notes and coins invented?

To make buying and selling fair and easier! In ancient times, people used barter system as a means of exchange. Over time, this system created problems for people. Like, wheat could be exchanged only when harvested, fruit only when ripened and that too before it got spoiled. Such issues with the commodities led people to create coins out of precious metals to use as money.

Find out!

What are the two sides of a coin called?

22 Why do debit cards have chips?

To make them more secure! Debit cards are made with a magnetic strip, which comprises all the information about an individual's bank account. To prevent the misuse of these cards, a chip was introduced. While the magnetic strip has the unchanging data of a person's bank account, the chip creates unique codes every time the card is used. So it's almost impossible to duplicate it.

Pocket fact

On the coin!
Romans were the first to stamp the image of a living person on a coin. They used Julius Caesar's image on a coin in 44 BCE.

Find out!

When is the World Braille Day celebrated?

23 Why do Braille cells have six dots?

So that they can fit on a fingertip! Braille is a system of reading and writing used by the visually impaired. It was invented by Louis Braille. Its characters are represented by patterns of raised dots that can be felt with the fingertips. Each Braille cell consists of six dots that are arranged in different patterns to make up letters of the alphabet, numbers and punctuation marks. The size, shape and positions of the 'Braille cell' were created by Louis Braille. Four dots did not give enough variations in dot placement, while eight dots were too large for a fingertip. So, the classic arrangement came to be six dots.

Pocket fact

Without a name!
Great Britain is the only country that prints stamps without its name on them. It was they who invented stamps!

24 Why were stamps invented?

To recover the cost of the mail! Before the invention of stamps, the person who received a mail had to pay for it. However, if the recipient was not available, or was unable or unwilling to pay for the mail, the cost of the mail was not recovered. To overcome this problem, postage stamps were invented. These stamps indicated that the mail bearing them had been paid for. The first-issued postage stamp called the British Penny Black Stamp was released in Great Britain in 1840.

25 Why were video games invented?

To increase TV sales! The first video game was invented after an engineer named Ralph H. Baer created the prototype for the world's first video game console. Baer worked for a television manufacturer. He came up with the idea to incorporate an electronic video game into a TV set to increase sales. The company rejected his plan, but Baer eventually developed a prototype console in 1967. This became the world's first video game console called Magnavox Odyssey.

Find out!

Why are mobile apps named so?

26 Why do we need to update apps?

Pocket fact

The 3DO was the first video game system that was based entirely on CD technology. It was introduced in 1993.

To update their security! You must have often noticed the 'update your app' notification on your mobile phone and computer. This indicates that the app you are using has been enhanced with new and improved features. By updating the app, you can ensure that your phone and computer are up-to-date and secure. When an app is updated, it fixes the existing bugs in the software. Major companies regularly update their apps because they want to fix the flaws in their app before hackers try to misuse them.

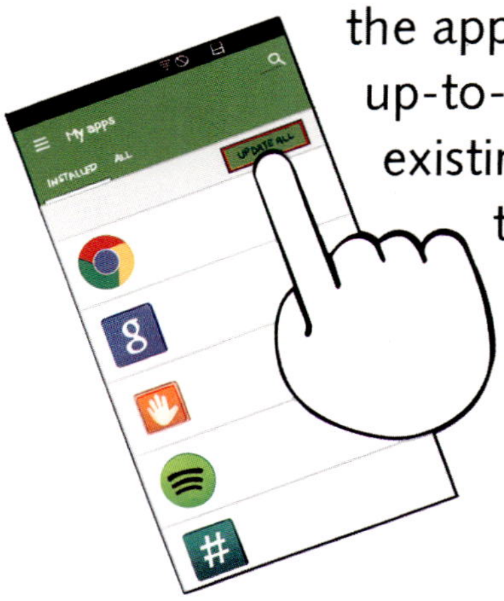

OTHER TITLES IN THIS SERIES